This book belongs to

Big Girls Don't Cry - Taking the Emotion out of Finances



Cover Design by Donna Osborn Clark at www.CreationByDonna.com

Photography by Larry V. Dalton

Typeset & Interior Design by www.CreationByDonna.com

ISBN: 978-0-615-64225-3

Money Wisdom for Women



Sacramento CA 95816

Printed in the Unites States of America



Big Girls Don't Cry Taking the Emotion out of Finances is published by *Anita R. Johnson of Money Wisdom for Women. Money Wisdom for Women* mission is to equip women with Wealth Building skills leaving a legacy for their children.

# Big Girls Don't Cry

## Taking the Emotion Out of Finances

Anita R. Johnson

ANITA R. JOHNSON
AND ASSOCIATES

## How to use this book to receive the best value?

As you begin to read this book, you will notice the value of the taking care of your finances. These simple concepts are so simple you soon forget they are simple.

Taking of your finances opens doors that you will soon find that are more beneficiation to the rest of your life.

Pull up a pen or pencil while reading and get stated to financial security,

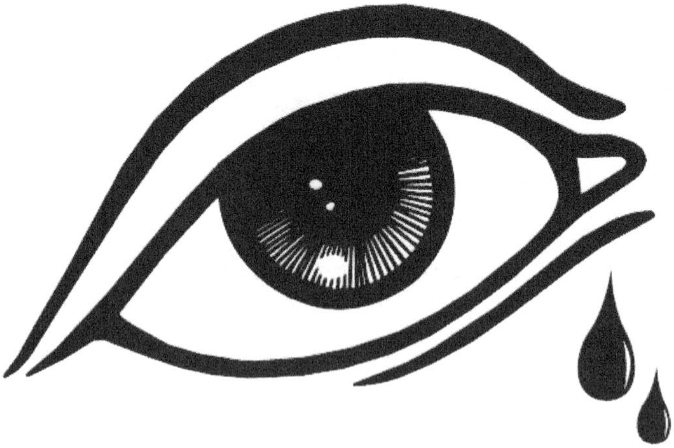

To my children Cordelia & Leonard, you have always been my inspiration for doing what I do. I love both of you greatly.

**MOM**

# Introduction

***Big Girls Don't Cry*** is an amazing journey that every woman should take in her life. I have walked this road many times. It is amazing and I am still here to talk and write about it.

***Big Girls Don't Cry*** touches women in a personal way as it discusses our true relationship with our finances, and how we allow so many distractions to interfere with us becoming financially secure.

Now is the time to free ourselves from bad habits, such as emotional shopping, unhealthy relationships, rescuing our adult children, low self-esteem, not caring, and allowing others to make financial decisions for us.

Once we are free from these and other poor financial habits we are free to create good financial habits such as emergency savings, retirement building, healthy shopping tips, healthy relationships, learning the difference between self-esteem, self-worth, and net worth. All of these habits build wealth, leading to a legacy for our children to follow and not leaving debt for them.

# Table of Contents

# Chapter 1

**My future depends on my present.**

*Test Your Knowledge*

## Test Your Knowledge

**OK let's begin with a quick test. I know! You don't like test, but this is a good test. Testing your financial knowledge gives you a clear understanding of where you are and how much more you need to learn. Remember I am about educating knowledge. If you don't know the answer, that's OK. You have the opportunity to test again.**

**My suggestion would be take the test on a separate sheet of paper at the beginning of this journey and again once you finish the book. See the difference.**

## Test Your Knowledge

1. How much of your Gross Income is paid in taxes?

2. What is the difference between Gross Income and Net Income?

3. "On Sale" means a "True Sale" Why? Why not?

4. What is the difference between a want and a need?

5. Who are the biggest consumers in America?

6. What is the percentage of couples that argue about money?

7. What percentage of your net income should be spent on housing?

8. Do you have concise clear financial goals?

## Test Your Knowledge

9. Do you know the three credit reporting agencies?

10. What is your greatest fear regarding money?

11. What did your parents teach about money?

12. Do you have an emergency savings?

13. Do you have a retirement savings plan?

14. How confident are you in your financial planner? Tax Planner?

15. Do you have an estate planner?

16. What is your memory of money?

## Test Your Knowledge

17. What do you consider your money success?

18. Do you track your spending?

19. Do you know your interest rate on your mortgage?

20. What is one thing you want to take away from this course that you will begin and continue to use in managing your finances?

**Notes**

**Notes**

**Notes**

**Notes**

# Chapter 2

**Recovery is a human right.**

*Gross Income*

## Gross Income

**Why did I put this here? I can hear what everyone is saying to me, I know the definition of gross income. I know what it looks like. I want you to take another look at your gross income. Women earn .77 cents to every man's dollar. My question is you earning enough to meet all your living needs. Right now is the time to find out.**

**The first pages ask you to look at your gross income, deduct any taxes, getting you to your net income. From your net income, deduct your living expenses.**

**Let's get to work.**

**Gross Income**

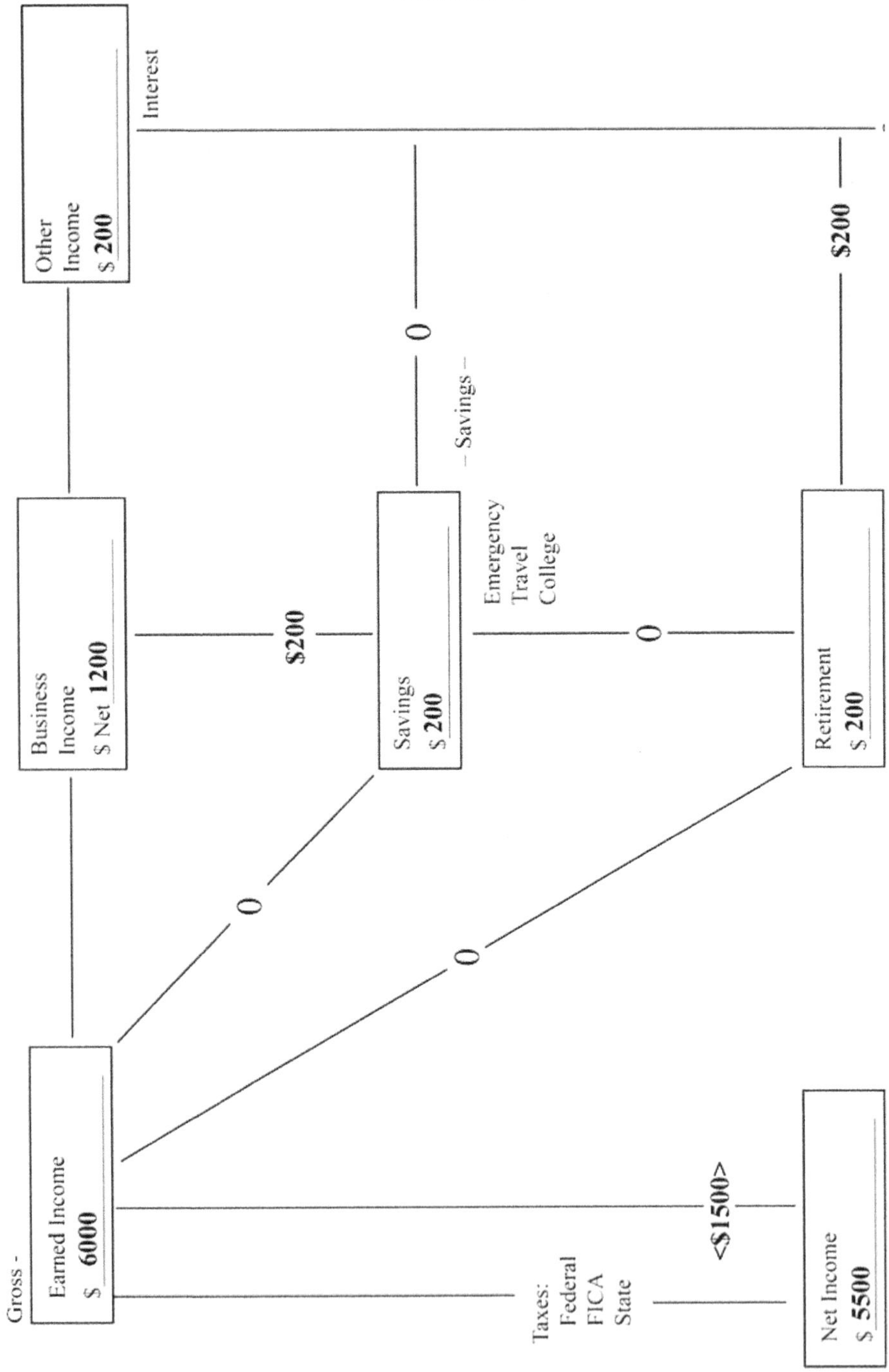

**Gross Income**

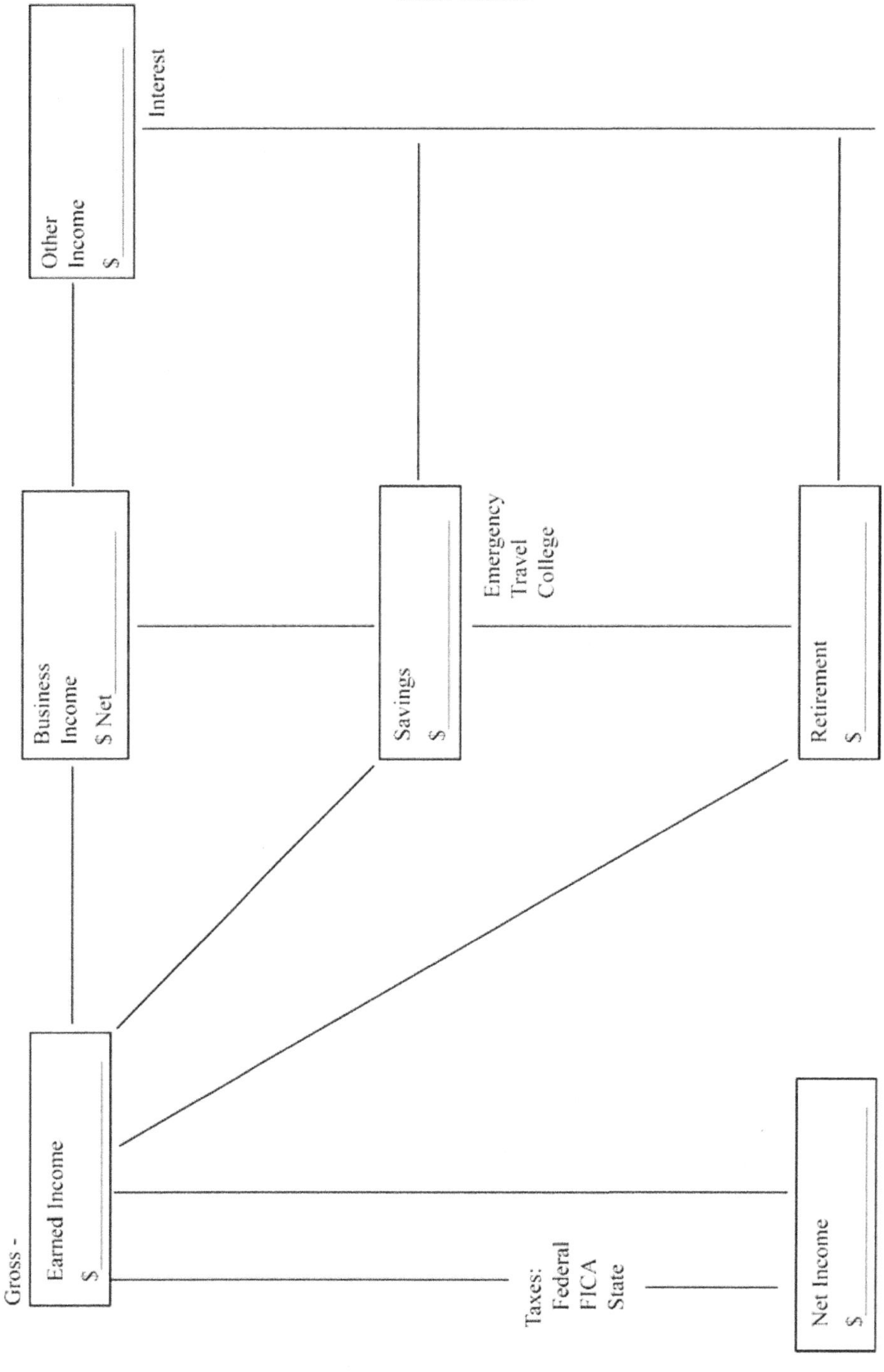

**Notes**

# Chapter 3

**To be what I am today, I had to be what I was yesterday.**

*Net Income*

## Net Income

**Here we are at net income. Net income is the amount you have left over after all the taxes are deducted from the gross income. From your net income you will deduct medical, rent/mortgage, insurances, car payment, union dues, retirement investments, food, clothing and other living expenses.**

**Why is this important? If you don't navigate a good gross income or increase you could be living above your means.**

**Here we go.**

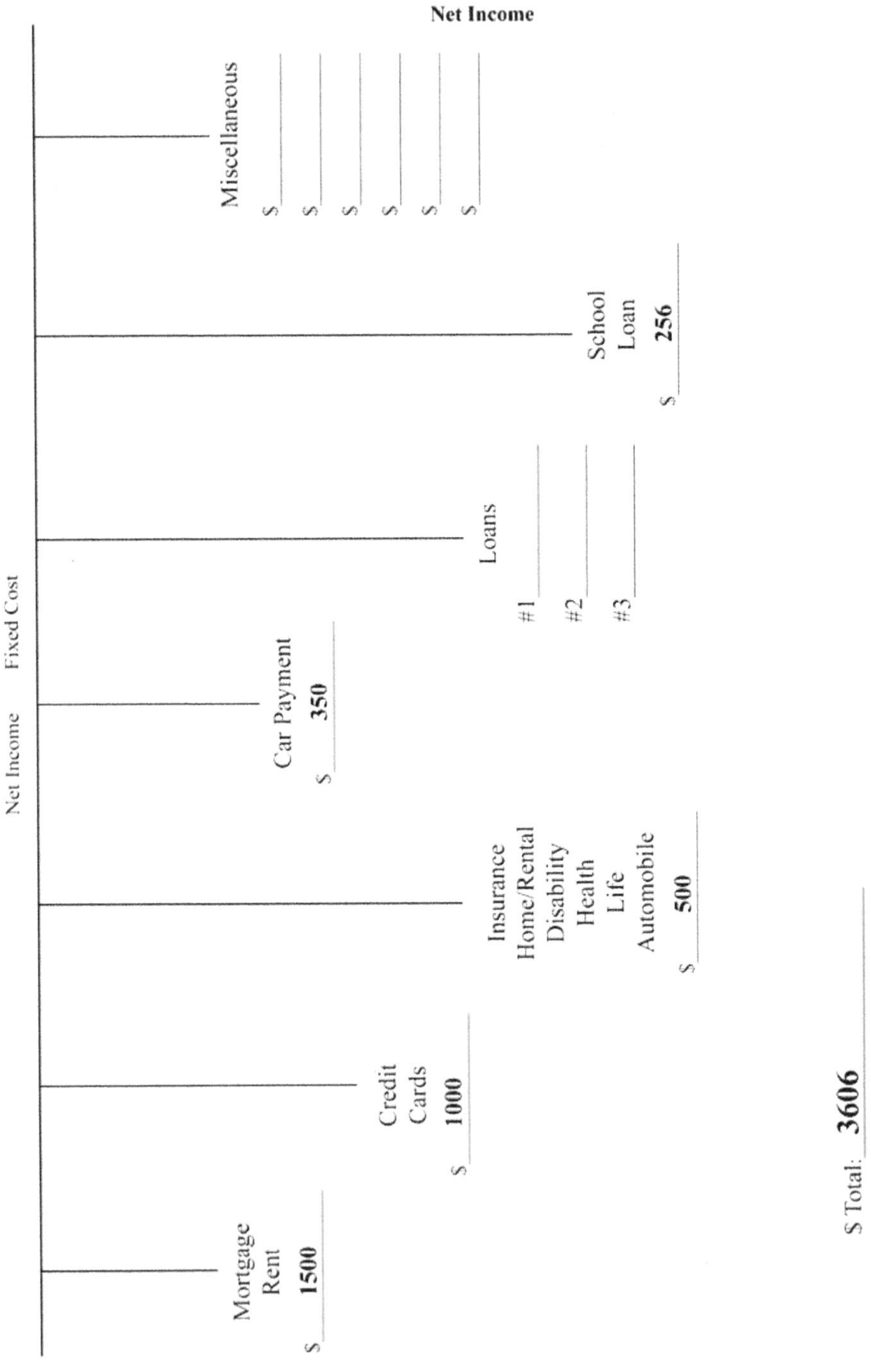
Net Income
Fixed Cost
Mortgage
Rent
$ 1500
Credit
Cards
$ 1000
Insurance
Home/Rental
Disability
Health
Life
Automobile
$ 500
Car Payment
$ 350
Loans
#1
#2
#3
School
Loan
$ 256
Miscellaneous
$
$
$
$
$
$
Net Income
$ Total: 3606

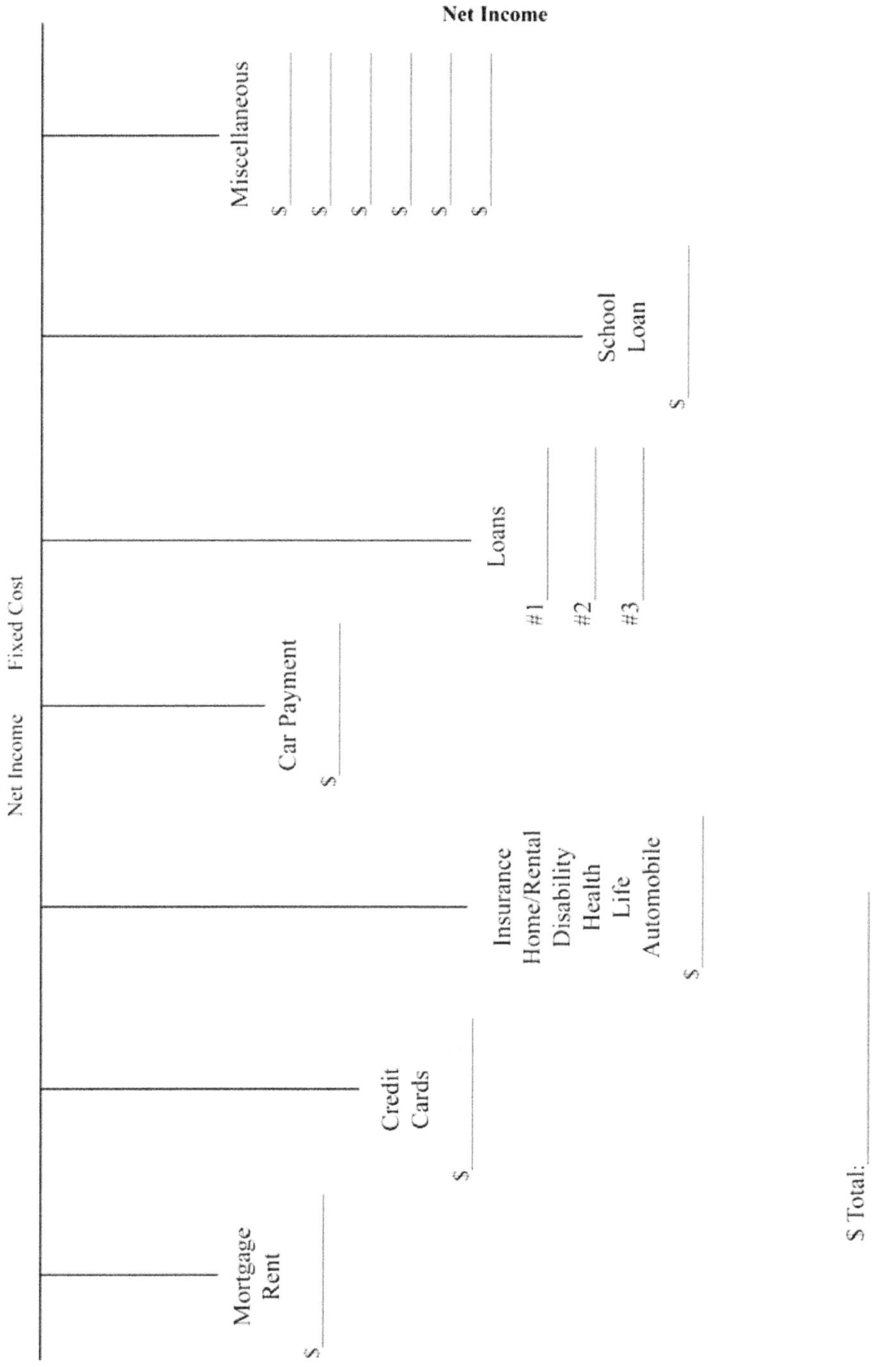
Net Income
Net Income
Fixed Cost
Mortgage
Rent
$
Credit
Cards
$
Insurance
Home/Rental
Disability
Health
Life
Automobile
$
Car Payment
$
Loans
#1
#2
#3
School
Loan
$
Miscellaneous
$
$
$
$
$
$
$ Total:

**Notes**

# Chapter 4

## Are you possessed by your possessions?

*Checking*

## Checking

**This age of prepaid cards, debit cards, online pay, and pay pal accounts, paying with checks disbursed through a checking account seems to be obsolete. I beg to differ. Using a checking account to pay bills gives you more control over your money. Example, you use your prepaid card to pay for utilities costing $125.00, the credit card servicer fee can be up to 20%; Total amount $130.00: if you decide to submit your payment through your checking account you will save $25.**

**The next pages gives understanding of how you can use your checking account to your benefit, helping you take control of your finances.**

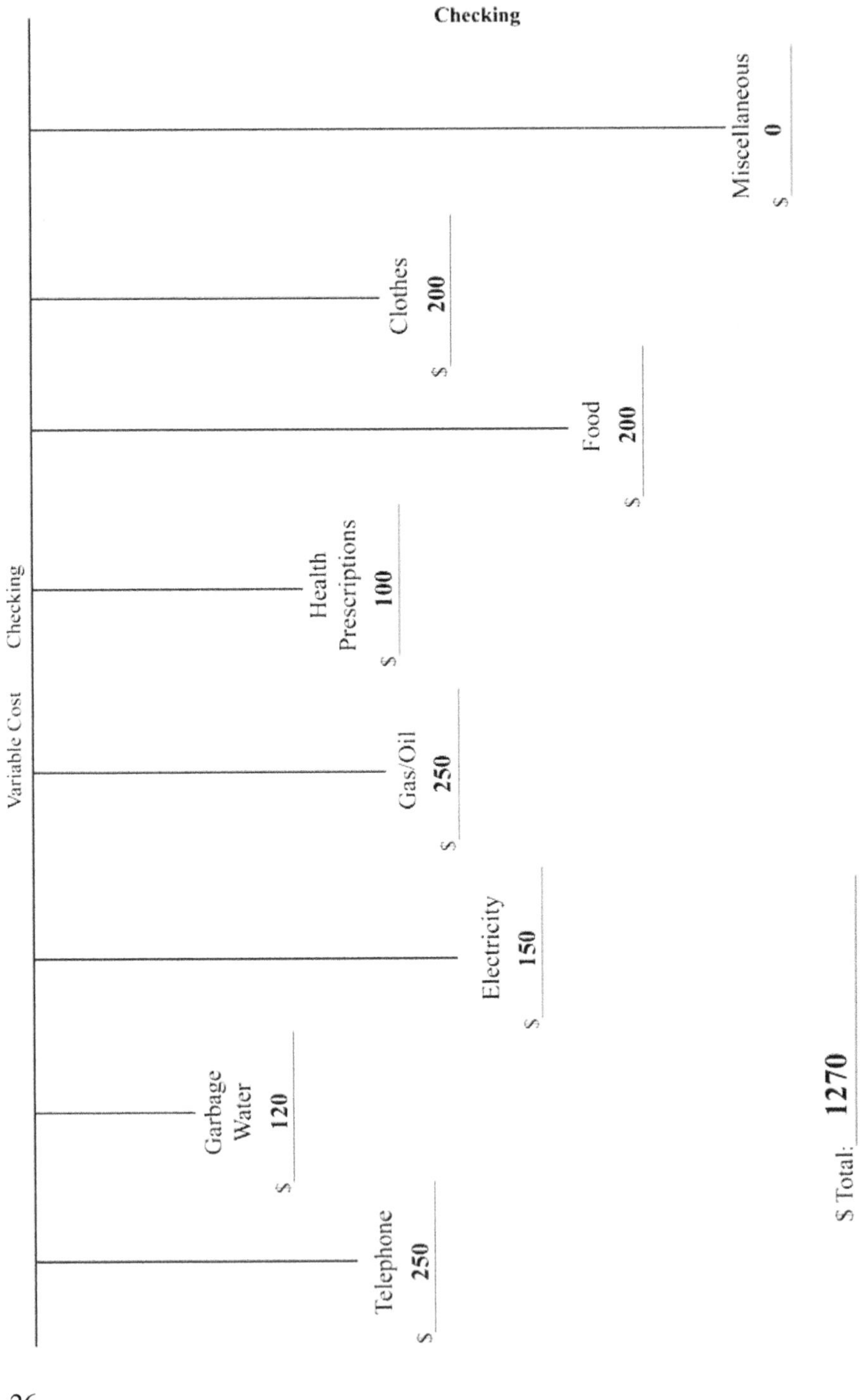
Checking
Variable Cost Checking
Telephone
$ 250
Garbage
Water
$ 120
Electricity
$ 150
Gas/Oil
$ 250
Health
Prescriptions
$ 100
Food
$ 200
Clothes
$ 200
Miscellaneous
$ 0
$ Total: 1270

**Checking**

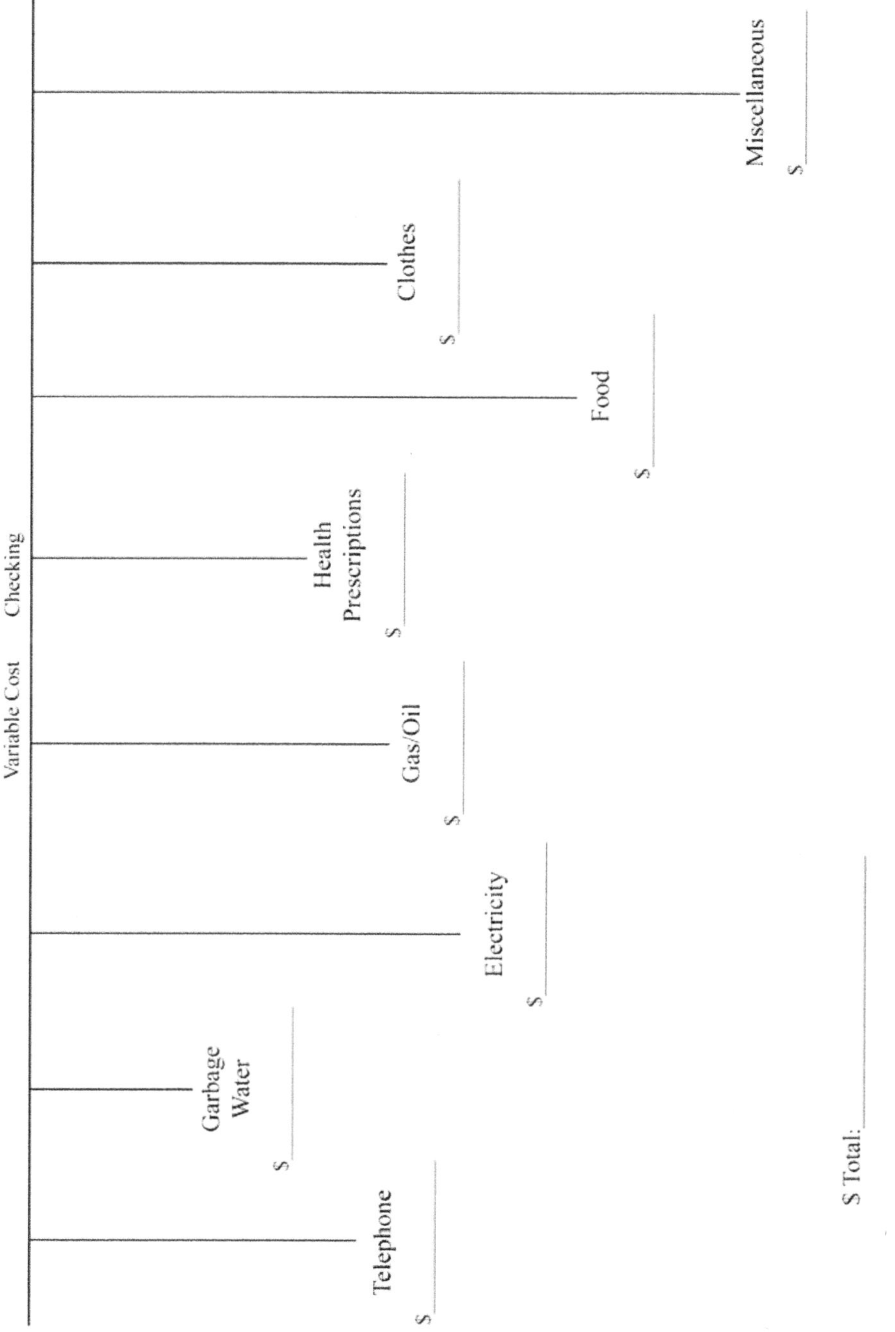
Variable Cost Checking
Telephone
$
Garbage
Water
$
Electricity
$
Gas/Oil
$
Health
Prescriptions
$
Food
$
Clothes
$
Miscellaneous
$
$ Total:

**Notes**

# Chapter 5

**I am responsible for me, financially, physically, and mentally.**

*Savings*

## Savings

**OH yes here it is, your savings account. What is in it? Nothing, I want to encourage you to saving. Begin with 3% of your net income going towards some type of saving. If you have not begun an emergency savings, begin. Do you want to travel? Designate some funds towards the travel fund.**

**Is it hard? Sure, of course, but if you begin with a small amount, even $5.00 it is more than you saved yesterday.**

**I am reminded of a story (true) of a woman years ago that would go to bank (when there were pass books) taking her nickels, dimes, quarters, pennies to deposit them. One day the teller said "Why do you bring such small amounts for deposit?" The woman replied "Look at the balance in my pass book." When the teller looked the woman had accumulated over $5,000 in her savings.**

**This can be you, with all the tools banks have now. Take advantage of the savings plan.**

**Savings**

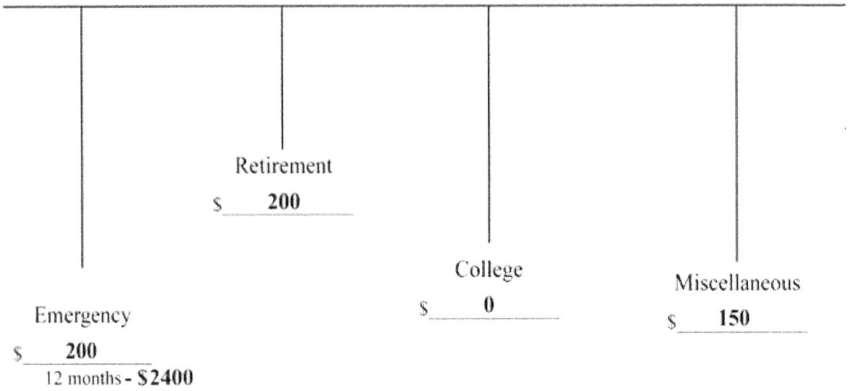


$ Total: **550**

**Savings**

Retirement

$____________

College

$____________

Miscellaneous

$____________

Emergency

$____________

12 months

$ Total:____________________

**Notes**

# Chapter 6

**Patience and persistence is being passionate.**

*Recipe for Financial Security*

## Recipe for Financial Security

**The recipe for financial freedom has only ten steps. You may have heard or seen them before; however, you might not have paid much attention to them at all. Today we will work through these ten steps which will become ten positive financial habits.**

### 1. Start Where You Are

**Beginning a journey takes courage, especially the financial journey. Start Where You Are. Put one foot in front of the other. Forget about the things you have done in the past concerning your finances. Today is a new day. List three things that can help you Start Where You Are!**

**1.** ______________________________

**2.** ______________________________

**3.** ______________________________

Notes

______________________________

______________________________

______________________________

______________________________

______________________________

______________________________

**Recipe for Financial Security**

**2. Make A Date With Your Finances**

**Remember when you met that special someone and you had your first date; how exciting was that! This is the same thing; Make A Date With Your Finances. You are now going to spend one day a week on a date with your finances. The reward for dating will be better organization, less debt, and an overall good feeling. List three days (dates) that you can spend with your finances.**

**1.** ______________________________

**2.** ______________________________

**3.** ______________________________

**Notes**

______________________________

______________________________

______________________________

______________________________

______________________________

______________________________

**Recipe for Financial Security**

**3. Create A Savings Plan**

**Do you have a savings plan? Most of us don't. We have no emergency plan, no travel emergency plan, no college savings plan, and no retirement plan. This is the time to begin a savings plan even if it is only 3 percent of your net income. List three types of savings plans you want to implement within six months.**

**1.** ____________________________________________

**2.** ____________________________________________

**3.** ____________________________________________

Notes

____________________________________________

____________________________________________

____________________________________________

____________________________________________

____________________________________________

____________________________________________

**Recipe for Financial Security**

**4. Develop a Financial Spending Plan (Formerly a Budget)**

**This is a hard one. Most of us dislike budgets. We will no longer use a budget. It will be called A Financial Spending Plan. Your goal here is to create a comfortable spending plan you and your family can live within. See attached spreadsheet.**

**1.** ____________________________________________

**2.** ____________________________________________

**3.** ____________________________________________

Notes

____________________________________________

____________________________________________

____________________________________________

____________________________________________

____________________________________________

____________________________________________

## Recipe for Financial Security

### 5. Know Your Weaknesses

**What do you mean know my weaknesses? I have no weaknesses. Oh yes, ego! Sometimes we think we can do it alone. There are some things we can do alone; however, tackling our finances is not one of them. We need professional help: financial planners, accountants, bankers, and tax experts. List three professionals that can help you.**

**1.** ______________________________

**2.** ______________________________

**3.** ______________________________

Notes

______________________________

______________________________

______________________________

______________________________

______________________________

______________________________

## Recipe for Financial Security

### 6. Develop A Wish List

**Wish upon a star as someone once said and you may get your wish. I want you to use your wishes in a different way, though. You'll be wishing on three items that you want to completely eliminate from your spending plan. List three financial items that you want to completely eliminate this year.**

**1.** ______________________________

**2.** ______________________________

**3.** ______________________________

Notes

______________________________

______________________________

______________________________

______________________________

______________________________

______________________________

**Recipe for Financial Security**

## 7. Be Realistic

**So I want to pay off all my credit card debt in six months, the car in one year, have an emergency savings of $10,000 in one year. Be Realistic about your plans! There is nothing more frustrating if you are making this journey through rose color glasses. List three financial goals along with dates you will achieve them.**

**1.** ______________________________________________

**2.** ______________________________________________

**3.** ______________________________________________

Notes

______________________________________________

______________________________________________

______________________________________________

______________________________________________

______________________________________________

______________________________________________

**Recipe for Financial Security**

**8. Be Disciplined**

**Discipline, what a great thing! In order to succeed in this journey you need discipline. Yes, there will be times that you want those shoes and you'll buy them; there will be times when you go to the movies; there will be times when you go to dinner. And I say do them, but not overdo them. Refer to your plans before you make a decision about shoes, movies, or dinner.**

**1.** ____________________

**2.** ____________________

**3.** ____________________

**Notes**

____________________

____________________

____________________

____________________

____________________

____________________

## Recipe for Financial Security

### 9. Stay Focused

**In order to stay disciplined, you must stay focused. Write your financial goals on paper; hang them up somewhere where you can see them. Once you have achieved one goal, celebrate; don't celebrate with charging more on the credit card because you are defeating yourself. Try something new like walking in the park or riding a skateboard. List three new things that can help you stay focused.**

**1.** ______________________________

**2.** ______________________________

**3.** ______________________________

**Notes**

______________________________

______________________________

______________________________

______________________________

______________________________

______________________________

**Recipe for Financial Security**

**10. Have Fun**

**Being on this financial journey may take awhile, but have fun as you go. Once reaching a financial goal, celebrate. Do something with the family or ride a bike; have fun. List three things that you can do to have fun while walking this financial journey.**

**1.** ____________________

**2.** ____________________

**3.** ____________________

**Notes**

____________________

____________________

____________________

____________________

____________________

____________________

# Chapter 7

**What will make your daily walk extra special?**
**Walk with God hand-in-hand.**

*Your Tracker*

# Anita's Tracker

Do you ever wonder where all your money goes? For one week, carry the Anita's Tracker with you and track where you spend your money. At the end of a week you'll have a clear idea of just where those extra dollars could be hiding.

In the future, you can use funds you currently fritter away to increase savings, pay off bills or buy something special.

| Item | Cost |
| --- | --- |
| *Example: Lunch at work* | *$5.87* |
| | |
| | |
| | |
| | |
| | |
| | |
| | |
| | |
| | |
| | |
| | |
| | |
| | |
| | |
| | |
| | |
| | |
| | |
| | |
| | |
| | |
| | |

Total ____________

# Summary

Developing this guide was fun for me. It was fun for me because I had to walk this journey alone. I had to figure out my financial goals, make a date with my finances, develop a wish list, create a spending plan, know my weaknesses, be realistic, be disciplined, stay focused, and have fun.

I decided to share my journey with others so that you don't have to reinvent the wheel. It is already invented for you.

# About the Author

Ms. Anita Renee Johnson, a native of Oakdale, Louisiana, has been passionate about finance for many years.

During her career, Ms. Johnson has developed and instructed numerous courses designed to assist all ages in making sound financial decisions. These courses include: *"Big Girls Don't Cry – Taking the Emotion Out of Finances", "Emotional & Financial Freedom", "Entrepreneur Planning", and "The Game of Life-Foster Youth."*

The most current project for Ms. Johnson is AR Johnson & Associates- *"Money Wisdom for Women"* Established in 1998, her goal is to provide sound financial advice to her clients. This information is offered either in one-on-one consulting sessions, workshops, seminars, or conferences. Through ARJ & Associates, Ms. Johnson and her team have counseled over two thousand businesses and individuals in personal and business finance. Their topics include: tax preparation and planning, estate planning, Money Wisdom – the Board Game, Money Wisdom for Small Businesses, pre-retirement for Federal Employees, specifically the Environmental Protection Agency, and Race to Retirement.

Ms. Johnson says: *"My commitment is to inform and educate my clients so that they can make sound financial decisions."*

**Connect with Ms. Johnson**
**www.moneywisdomforwomen.net**
**www.www.facebook.com/anitareneej**
**www.twitter.com/monewisdomwomen**
**www.ThePraiseHouse.com**
Tuesday & Thursday 1:00 PT Radio Broadcast
**www.Praise98.FM.com**
Friday 5:00 P.T.
**www.anitareneejohnson@typepad.com**
**www.linkedin.com/in/anitarjohnson**

# Services

Personal Financial Planning

Small Business Financial Planning

Financial Seminars

VIP Financial Days

Financial Workshops

Broadcasting of Financial Advice Through Radio

Estate-Planning

Membership Packages Available

Connect: Money Wisdom for Women
3104 O Street Suite 315
Sacramento CA 95816
916-452-4270

**Have Anita R. Johnson Speak at Your Next Event.**

Ms. Johnson is available for your next event as a keynote speaker or breakout session.

For more information
Email us at: shields.networkpr@gmail.com

The road to recovery is paved with love, peace, hope, and understanding.

Made in the USA
Monee, IL
04 November 2026

67374804R00039